To my Texas friend Pat

[signature]

America's First Warriors
Native Americans and Iraq

PHOTOGRAPHS AND TEXT BY **Steven Clevenger**

Museum of New Mexico Press   Santa Fe

Sing your death song and die like a hero going home.

—Tecumseh, Shawnee chief

Introduction: America's First Warriors

Steven Clevenger

In October 2006, I attended a yellow-ribbon welcoming-home ceremony in Rio Rancho, New Mexico, for the 116th Transportation Company, New Mexico National Guard, based at Gallup, New Mexico. The men and women of the unit had just returned from a yearlong deployment to Iraq. Despite the ubiquitous IEDs that Iraq harbors, the 116th came home with all its members intact.

I attended the ceremony with the idea of documenting Native American soldiers—or warriors as they call themselves. As a photojournalist, I have covered seven wars. My career began in 1971 in Cambodia, where I turned twenty-two. I feel that this background allows me to examine the Native American warrior culture with the perspective of someone who knows what it is to willingly participate in and survive a war.

With this book, I want to explain the warrior culture to non–Native Americans and perhaps attract the interest of natives who have lost their culture and encourage them to examine

A woman shows her allegiance to both her active-duty son and her veteran husband, who has just returned from a yearlong deployment to Iraq. A homecoming parade was held in Rio Rancho, New Mexico, in November 2006.

what they have lost. I hope the book will also prove useful to the military, in that those in command may develop a greater understanding of their Native American subordinates—what motivates them to serve and why some engage in ancient ceremonies.

At the yellow-ribbon ceremony, I first photographed Native American families waiting for veterans to arrive and made conversation with a number of them. Soon a convoy of trucks bearing the returning soldiers appeared. The crowd was ecstatic to see their friends and relatives after the yearlong separation. I photographed the joy-filled meetings. After the initial reunions, I approached a family I had spoken with earlier. It was the family of Sergeant Bradley Henio, returning from his third deployment to Iraq. Bradley and his family invited me to a welcoming-home/cleansing ceremony to be held at the Ramah Reservation Chapter House a few weeks later.

From that initial meeting and the following ceremony, contacts and events continued. At the cleansing ceremony, where I conducted my first recorded interview, I met Bradley's father, World War II veteran Bailey Henio. Later I traveled to his home on the Navajo Reservation and made my second interview.

After investigating which National Guard units had significant numbers of Native Americans, I made arrangements to travel to Iraq in September 2007 and to embed with Company A, Second Battalion, 200th Infantry Division, New Mexico National Guard. Company A included more than forty Native Americans—both men and women—of various tribes and pueblos.

In May 2007, I first made contact with Company A at its Rio Rancho armory. The soldiers were preparing to leave New Mexico for Fort Dix, New Jersey, where they would receive further training before deploying to Iraq. I held a meeting with the Native Americans in the company, explained my project, and asked their permission to document them during the Iraq deployment. I encountered some skepticism but also a lot of interest.

Later that week, Company A had a yellow-ribbon ceremony and left New Mexico. I left that same day for Osage County, Oklahoma, where my own tribe, the Osage, was to hold its annual War Mothers' Dance. The low-key yet significant dance is held to honor veterans of the Osage tribe. At this ceremony, I made contacts that led to more interviews with veterans.

In September I caught up with Company A in Iraq. There I got to know a number of native soldiers. I began to photograph and interview those interested in participating.

Upon my return to the States, I continued to search for and research the warrior culture. When Company A returned to New Mexico, I was there to greet them along with their families and friends. Like the 116th Transportation Company, this New Mexico National Guard unit also returned intact. By now my interviewees had become friends, and I was invited to celebrations for their return. One invited me to a traditional Pueblo dinner. Another extended an invitation to a warrior dance to be held in his honor. From these experiences, I learned much about the motivation and beliefs behind the warrior culture—some of it expected, some not.

The definition of a warrior for Native Americans has basically remained the same since pre-Columbian times. A warrior is the protector of his people. Strength, honor, pride, devotion, wisdom, and spiritual toughness are required to fulfill that duty. Coincidentally, the Native American warrior code is similar to the code of the U.S. Army. Both groups value loyalty, duty, respect, selfless service, honor, integrity, and personal courage. Requirements for a successful U.S. military career—strength, bravery, pride, and wisdom—match those for the warrior.

Even though they weren't granted citizenship until 1924, Native Americans have served in all of America's wars. During World War I, 12,000 Native Americans served. World War II saw 44,000 serve out of a total native population of 350,000. Forty-two thousand natives served in Vietnam. In proportion to their numbers in the population, Native Americans participate in military service more than any other ethnic group. According to a story that has been attributed to a number of different tribes, when Congress passed the World War II conscription bill, a member of the Blackfoot tribe said, "Since when has it been necessary for Blackfeet to draw lots to fight?" The entire football team at the Santa Fe Indian School volunteered for the military after their 1942 homecoming game.

An obvious question concerning Native American service in the U.S. military is: Why should a people who have suffered so horribly at the hands of the U.S. government defend that government? Answers to the question vary. One is this: We were never conquered. Tricked, duped maybe. But not defeated. Our culture survived.

One native veteran proclaimed that his military professionalism prevented him from giving much consideration to the question. Another native veteran said he was not defending the U.S. government but the land of his people. Yet another veteran replied, "I feel it is an honor to defend what is America now. Because it is where our people and where my family resides. Therefore, I am still carrying on the tradition that was passed on to us, which is to defend our homeland. That aspect hasn't changed. Whether it is an American flag or a camp circle of lodges." Another reply: "The Native American was the only one who was actually fighting for his country that belonged to him in the beginning."

Reasons for following the military road or going to war also vary. Many native veterans speak of wanting the esteem showed to their own veteran fathers by other tribal members. Some mention a desire to continue the warrior culture, as well as wanting to develop a respect for native culture among nonnatives. A more easily understood reason for many is that war offers a way to earn feathers and to face the enemy. More simply put, it offers a way to become a man or a warrior.

Native veterans also talk about service—service to the community, service to the family, service to the tribe, service to the people, service to the country. To some extent, natives are encouraged to join the military. Osage tribal member John Henry Mashunkashey explains, "Because in our way of life, a warrior is the combat leader. He becomes a leader not only in the military, but he becomes a leader for your tribe. Just knowing that this man here was in a situation sometimes where it took life or death becomes an asset for the tribe—to know that they can turn to him and say, 'We got to do this, and how can we do this, and what is the best solution?'"

When I started researching this book, I formed a thesis of what I expected to find and convey to the reader. I thought that because of native traditions—encouragement of the warrior culture and tribal rites both before and after military service—native veterans would have an easier time readapting to life after the military than nonnatives. I thought that returning native veterans wouldn't suffer as much or at all from post-traumatic stress disorder, which has caused so much suffering among so many veterans.

But this turned out not to be the case. While the ceremonies, prayers, and medicine help, native veterans still pay a high price. Often, the PTSD begins before they leave for war. It begins at home on the reservation. Trauma exists in the extreme poverty found on most reservations. It exists in the form of drug addiction and alcoholism. It exists in high suicide rates and family disfunction. Underfunded health services add to this trauma. Most of the veterans photographed for this book suffer from PTSD.

Acceptance by their tribes helps. The recognition of their service and the honors offered to them help. The traditional cleansing ceremonies help. Modern counseling and drug therapy also offer solace. The Department of Veterans Affairs even offers programs for Native American veterans who suffer from PTSD and other maladies. But despite the acceptance, honors, ceremonies, and government programs, the trauma of wartime experiences remains.

Perhaps the most famous modern Native American warrior, Ira Hayes, is the saddest example of a warrior unable to make the transition back to peacetime. Despite being acclaimed and honored for his participation in raising the American flag over Iwo Jima during World War II, he turned to alcohol and died, frozen in a ditch, less than ten years later. Not all stories have happy endings.

Throughout U.S. history, until passage of the American Indian Religious Freedom Act of 1978, the U.S. government attempted to suppress native religious practices. Missionaries tried to convert the native population to Christianity. Yet many native people continued to practice their traditional religious beliefs and ceremonies. Even among those brought up as Christians, traditional beliefs are still important to their understanding of life, health, and illness. Native warriors especially depend upon ancient ceremonies and prayers that offer protection and healing.

Different tribes offer their warriors different protective ceremonies before they leave for war. The Osage send their warriors off with the prayers of their peers, while the Navajo give departing warriors medicine bundles. The bundles are a source of protection and spiritual power. They contain sacred items, such as corn pollen, which represents life. When World War II veteran Bailey Henio left for duty in the European theater, his grandfather—himself a Navajo warrior who had fought against U.S. forces, Pueblos, and Mexicans—gave him a protective ceremony and a medicine bundle containing corn pollen and a small white feather from a live eagle. Bailey's grandfather told him to throw the feather into the air if he were captured, and this would enable him to escape. During Bailey's first experience in war, on June 6, 1944, at Omaha Beach, his medicine bundle became soaked in the ocean. But Bailey continued to carry it throughout the war, including during the Battle of the Bulge, when he was surrounded by German forces. Luckily, Bailey never needed to test the power of the feather. When he returned to the Navajo Reservation, his grandfather removed the contents of the bundle and scattered them around the home to ensure good things for the family.

In the past, returning warriors were kept separate from the rest of the tribe, so as not to infect other members with the bad experiences or spirits they might have brought home. Today that separation is not enforced. In addition, ceremonies that once lasted for days have been shortened. Some ceremonies are closed to all but the veteran's family and the medicine man, while others are open to the community.

Sweat lodge ceremonies are common in many tribes. Cheyenne Bill Cody Ayon says:

In my tribe, the sweat lodge is the oldest ceremony in its purist form that is still in use today. The cleansing aspect of it is purely spiritual. Not only does the heat and the steam from the stones cleanse your body by opening your pores, but it releases any bad thoughts that you might have in your mind. You can feel this tension or this weight on your shoulders that combat or deployments might have put on a service member, and it helps release that. And it also helps if the soldier or service member is leaving home. It helps reassure them with all those that are sacrificing and being in that sweat lodge with them, the family members, praying for them. It reassures that God is going with you. That the thoughts and prayers of your loved ones are also with you at all times. It makes the service member that much more competent as a working part of the military. Because they have so much support and so much love at home that when they step foot onto that foreign soil or do whatever their country asks of them, they are willing and able to do that.

War songs are also used to honor returned warriors. Songs can honor an individual, a battle, or a war. At Camp Cropper in Iraq, a drumming group made of Native Americans from a New Mexico National Guard unit sang of their experiences. Herb Adson, a Pawnee lead singer, told about a Desert Storm song. The lyrics included the line "Saddam Hussein, we spilled your blood." Sometimes relatives commission songs for their returned warriors. Once a song is made, it is the property of the honored veteran and can be sung only with his or her permission.

When individuals are raised in the warrior culture, they leave for war knowing that the tribe supports them. As Bill Cody Ayon said in his interview:

When you come from a society or a family like mine, where they raise you in this fashion, where they honor you to be in the military and serve your country, that's what you are supposed to do. To defend this country and defend your tribe and defend your people and your land. You are supposed to do that. You are supposed to give yourself for the betterment of the people and the betterment of man. I feel that when you go into something with that mind-set, you are light-years above a young man who might come into the service and say, "I did this for college money."

When John Henry Mashunkashey came home from Vietnam, he returned to a people who welcomed him and a country that didn't. He wasn't alone. While photographing the welcoming-home ceremony for Bradley Henio and other Iraq War veterans, I received this note:

What a contrast! When we Vietnam veterans (remember us? From that other unpopular war . . .) came home there was no ceremony, no welcome committee no acknowledgment or thanks of any kind. The only reception I remember was the antiwar protesters spitting (even trying to urinate on us) chanting and harassing us. Even remembering all that I love my country, I respect the office of our commander in chief and proud of our military and our proud men & women in uniform. With tears in my eyes I welcome you home—all you/us veterans.

Staff Sergeant Tyra Nakai, New Mexico National Guard
Interviewed February 7, 2009, Bernalillo, New Mexico

I did a lot of praying. I did a lot of praying. I think a lot of us did. You know, Navajos, we pray with the corn pollen. And there are certain ways you have to do it. My grandmother had taught me that before I left. Just to make sure, to keep me safe. On top of my regular prayers.

Prologue

My name is Bill Cody Ayon. I'm Tsitsistas, Southern Cheyenne, a human being.

I was brought up and given language, customs, and songs that honor those who have given their service to America's military, to my tribe, and to all indigenous people.

It is with this background that I follow the military road—like my father, my uncles, and my ancestors before me. To serve my family, my tribe, and my country is the greatest honor of all. Tradition has mandated this for me—from the echoes of warriors from the Little Bighorn to Iwo Jima to the streets of Baghdad. I thank them for their sacrifice.

The native tribes throughout America prepare us for our role and give support to those of us who face harm for their benefit. Blessing ceremonies from each tribe differ in name and function, but all serve as a cultural base, a foundation of strength.

My road here was no different. I participated in sacred ceremonies and prayer, and in our sacred sweat lodge. Those closest to me sent me off on deployment with their sacrifice and support.

Lieutenant Bill Cody Ayon stands by a Deming Police Department cruiser. Ayon is a lieutenant with both the New Mexico National Guard and the Deming Police Department.

As a boy and young man, I participated in gourd dances. This style of dance and song honors all veterans, from every branch of service, Native Americans or not. It is in this way and fashion that we native people choose to continue, to recognize those who serve in our country's military.

The Cheyenne military societies included the following groups of warriors: the Fox Society, the Elk Society, the Bow String Society, and the Dog Soldiers. They gave all so that I can stand here today, just as every Native American gives all today for America's freedoms and for the continuation of our culture.

Upon my return home, I will follow a new road. I will join the Tail Dance Society, a military society made up of veterans from every branch of service and tribal affiliation. This society commemorates service to tribe, service to community, and service to country, and it honors those who serve in our nation's military.

I would like to remind everyone that no matter what tribe, ethnicity, or cultural affiliation you belong to, service to your country is the greatest honor of all.

—From the Native American Appreciation Month ceremony,
Al Faw Palace, Camp Victory, Iraq, November 9, 2007

America's First Warriors

At a yellow-ribbon sending-off ceremony, World War II Navajo code talker Robert Walley stands before assembled members of the New Mexico National Guard. The code talkers devised and transmitted a secret code based on the Navajo language during World War II.

Specialist William Estevan, New Mexico National Guard
Interviewed in 2008, Camp Cropper, Iraq

My name is Specialist William Estevan III. I come from the pueblo of Acoma. I'm twenty-two years old right now. This is my second time out here in Iraq. The first tour I was in was at Camp Taji. That was in 2004–2005. I also had a protective ceremony before I came over that time too. So when we have a ceremony like that, it protects us through the whole time we are gone, till we get back home. The protective ceremony has to be undone. So that way we can be back with our family. So we can be purified from everything we had on us when we left home. So when I go back home, everything that I endured here, that I took in, I have to say a blessing for myself. And leave what I can back here. When I go back home, we get the full ceremony to where nothing is going to bother us after that.

There is a certain prayer that is said for an individual that is going off to war or going off to do something that may put harm to their body or soul or anything that may throw us off our path of goodness. It protects us from going in a certain direction, keeps us from going off the road, in other words. It keeps our mind clear. When that happens, we are told to say certain prayers. Throw our cornmeal. And say our morning prayer to the sun. When the sun comes up in the morning, we are supposed to greet the sun and say our prayers in the morning. In the evening time, that's pretty much until we get back home, and that's when we say our prayer in the evening: We are done with everything. Everything comes off us. It's just like a uniform. When you are done with everything, you take it off, and it's like relaxation.

When I came over the first time I didn't expect to be in so much danger. I didn't know what to expect. I was just expecting to do a job and go back home. My first convoy—I was with the Taos unit, 115th Transportation Company—there were only two other guys, and we got ambushed on our first convoy. Pretty soon we started hearing pops, and our commander said, "They're shooting at us." So that is what it sounds like; we'd never heard it before; we didn't expect it to sound like firecrackers. It was something I'll never forget.

Everyone has stories how it happened. I heard stories from my dad when he was in Vietnam, and from my brother when he was in Kosovo. I really went bad into drinking. It seems like a lot of military guys go through. It seems that Native Americans pick alcohol as their substitute for feeling better. And it's not. I went down that road. My dad went down that road. My brother Chris went down that same road, too. It seems the same trail that everybody goes down when they come back from a war. It's not the right way, but who is to say it's the wrong way either. My best advice to Native Americans is find something that you love so much and go toward it, don't go toward alcohol. Too many Native Americans who have gone to war, not even just gone to war but have gone to a place where they are gone from their families for so long—it drives them crazy. They just need to find something better than alcohol to go towards.

Two Native American soldiers, Specialist Alex Blueeyes (left) and Specialist Bobby Yazza (right), goofing at a yellow-ribbon ceremony for deploying New Mexico National Guard members at the armory in Rio Rancho. The two men are both Navajo tribal members.

Specialist Paula Kionut (Navajo) poses for a photograph with her niece during the pre-deployment yellow-ribbon ceremony at the Rio Rancho National Guard Armory in Rio Rancho, New Mexico.

Sergeant Frank Edison, a Navajo twice deployed to Iraq, holds his young son during a yellow-ribbon ceremony for Company A, Second Battalion, 200th Infantry Division, New Mexico National Guard. The following day, the company left for further training and later deployment to Iraq.

Right: Specialist Bobby Yazza prepares for deployment to Iraq at the yellow-ribbon ceremony.

Sergeant Dominick La Fontaine, New Mexico National Guard
Interviewed 2008 at Camp Cropper, Iraq

My name is Dominick G. La Fontaine. My unit is Alpha Company, First Battalion, 200th Infantry, New Mexico National Guard, out of Rio Rancho, New Mexico.

I've been in the National Guard for five years now, after a break in service. As far as the military is concerned, I'm pushing fourteen years now. I'm on active duty from seventeen to about twenty-six, twenty-seven years old. I'm thirty-seven now.

About the only thing I know about the warrior tradition is this photograph of my grandfather, photograph of my uncle. Your uncles, in just the way you are raised, influence your life. Being rough, being pushed around, getting whipped. Taught to be a man I guess, taught to be a male and to have that spirit—I hate to say warlike, but to be manly is what you call it. And that is how I affiliate being in the military, have some sense of military bearing related to the Navajo tribe.

Sergeant Dominick La Fontaine (Navajo) holds his son during the yellow-ribbon ceremony at the armory in Rio Rancho, New Mexico.

Sergeant Frank Edison stands in front of a sign warning Iraqi visitors to Camp Victory to behave themselves.

FOLLOW
INSTRUCTIONS OF
SOLDIERS
اتبع تعليمات الجنود
DEADLY FORCE
AUTHORIZED
قوة مخولة بالقتل

Left: Sergeant Frank Edison gestures to another guard while screening Iraqi visitors waiting to enter Camp Victory to meet with detained relatives. His job is to perform the initial screening of visitors.

Armed members of the Iraqi Provisional Volunteers staff a checkpoint south of Baghdad.

Left: A released Iraqi detainee joyfully leaves custody. Earlier he had pledged not to participate in the insurgency and to obey laws. The release coincides with Ramadan. The detention facility is at Camp Victory, south of Baghdad.

Iraqis wait in line to approach U.S. soldiers. The soldiers will check their paperwork before allowing them to visit with detained relatives. Visitors must perform a self-pat-down before approaching the guard station. This process prevents suicide bombers from injuring troops.

Before being allowed to approach U.S. soldiers and an Iraqi interpreter, a visitor must pat down her child to show that he isn't wearing an explosive belt. Other visitors wait their turn to present appointment papers and pass through the checkpoint. After being searched, visitors travel by bus to the visitor center, where detainees are brought to meet them.

Right: An Iraqi family waits to be called forward to a guard station before visiting a detainee. The mother shields her children with the necessary papers. Visits last one hour and can take weeks to arrange.

As a man presents paperwork to an Iraqi translator, his child eyes a U.S. soldier.

Members of the First Squadron, Third Brigade
Combat Team, Charlie Company, carefully
move up the stairs of a house said to contain
weapons. The information proved to be bogus.

Iraqi men sit against a wall, waiting to be released, while a U.S. soldier with H Company, Fourth Brigade, Second Infantry Division, examines a map. The company's mission is part of Operation Iron Harvest in Diyala Province.

Right: While on patrol in eastern Baghdad, a soldier pauses beside graffiti painted on a bullet-scarred wall.

A U.S. soldier from the First Squadron, Thirty-third Cavalry Regiment, scans the eye of an Iraqi man in the town of al-Dhour, south of Baghdad. The scanning device, known as HIIDE (handheld interagency identity detection equipment), is used to create a database of Iraqi men. The device also copies fingerprints.

A member of H Company, Fourth Brigade, Second Infantry Division, takes a break toward the end of a long day of operating inside the insurgent haven of Diyala Province. The unit is part of Operation Iron Harvest.

While on patrol in Anbar Province, two U.S. soldiers—one a chaplain—speak and play with an Iraqi child.

Below: U.S. soldiers hand out Iraqi flags to children in a Baghdad market.

Above: Attracted by a passing U.S. Army patrol, an Iraqi boy interacts with a U.S. soldier. The soldier is attached to the Second Cavalry Regiment, Fourth Squadron, Pale Horse Troop. The Baghdad neighborhood was the site of a controlled explosion the day before. A cache of hidden weapons was found and destroyed.

A U.S. soldier speaks with Iraqi children during a patrol in Anbar Province.

A member of the First Squadron, Third Brigade Combat Team, stands guard while fellow soldiers search for unexploded ordnance left from the beginning of the war. The date palm grove is near the Iraqi city of Abu Jasim.

U.S. forces based just four miles from the border of Iran, near Camp Normandy in Diyala Province.

A U.S. soldier writes a letter on a balcony over-
looking the manmade lake surrounding Saddam Hussein's Al Faw Palace. The U.S. military
uses the opulent palace as a command center.

Lieutenant Bill Cody Ayon speaks at a Native American Appreciation Month ceremony held at Saddam Hussein's main palace, Al Faw, at Camp Victory, Iraq.

Below: Lieutenant Bill Cody Ayon and other members of a drumming and singing group formed at Camp Cropper, Iraq. The soldiers were deployed from September 2007 to March 2008.

Specialist William Estevan (Acoma Pueblo) during drumming/singing practice at Camp Cropper, Iraq.

Specialist Paula Kionut sings during group practice at Camp Cropper, Iraq.

52

Lieutenant Bill Cody Ayon, New Mexico National Guard
Interviewed September 16, 2007, Camp Cropper, Iraq

These ceremonies and returning ceremonies are to cleanse the person before they leave, so they know that they are supported at home, which makes their job a little bit easier when they leave. And also when they return home as a purification rite, showing that all the bad they've seen or all the hurt they have felt or all the evil that surrounded them in whatever portion of the world they may have been in, or what situation they may have been in, is left behind. Like one of my uncles used to say, "It follows them like a shadow cast off. It's behind them now."

By all the family coming together and helping send you off this way, and helping you come back in the same fashion, returning the same way, it reassures the service member he's not alone in this fight. Because when a warrior goes off, he goes off to defend his way of life, to defend what is our culture, what is deemed our way of being, our way of living. And when he returns, he needs to be brought back into that circle, into that light. By having all people around him support him in this manner, it's a cleansing aspect.

We sing Dog Soldier songs in the sweat lodge. Dog Soldier songs are very old. They were passed on to my father and his wife. And these songs are sung in times of great need, and great strength is needed to do something like this. My father and his wife sing these songs for me in the sweat lodge, so that I will have the courage to do what I have to do. Also, we sing many songs in the sweat for strength, for endurance that we'll need in the days to come.

When I stepped off to leave from our home and came over on this deployment, I was blessed with my father's eagle fan, and he said prayers over me with my family around me in a circle. And I feel that power that is created from their love and appreciation of what I'm doing, and from what other service members are doing.

I feel it is an honor to defend what is America now. Because it is where our people and where my family resides. Therefore, I am still carrying on the tradition that was passed on to us, which is to defend our homeland. That aspect hasn't changed. Whether it is an American flag or a camp circle of lodges. That unique representation has always been there inside me. To me there is no irony in that. There is only honor in defending what is yours, what is your way of life. The old ones did that because they felt they were being encroached upon and their lifestyle was threatened. The way they thought the world to be was threatened. So they fought for their very lives against overwhelming odds. And that is to be honored. As we see throughout history that people are subdued, or conquered if you will. But their spirit never is. The spirit of that culture never is. I don't think there is a Cheyenne today that will tell you that we were conquered. I won't tell you that, and I don't expect any other Cheyenne to tell you that. Tricked, duped, maybe. That is a whole different ball of wax. But no, I feel no irony in defending my country and defending my way of life and my people and my family. I feel no irony in that. Like I said, I see only honor. And I'm glad to see my people still respect that. Whether it's a warrior for the United States flag or it's a warrior for the Cheyenne people. That is what it is to be honored. That is what it is to be a warrior.

We as Cheyenne people aren't going out to pick a fight. But when you come pick a fight, we bring a fight. And that is what I love about our culture. And whether you believe it or not, that is the same culture that America is built on. And I think that is why Native Americans hold close to that ideal.

I think that when you come from a society or a family like mine, where they raise you in this fashion, where they honor you to be in the military and serve your country, that's what you are supposed to do. To defend this country and defend your tribe and defend your people and your land. You are supposed to do that. You are supposed to give yourself for the betterment of the people and the betterment of man. I feel that when you go into something with that mind-set, you are light-years above a young man who might come into the service and say, "I did this for college money."

When you have eighteen years behind you, your family telling you every day, this is how a warrior is, these are the people you come from, look at the battles they fought, look at the trials they faced. You can stand up in front of a person like that and say, "This isn't that big of a deal." And when I return home, I'll be a stronger man because of it.

I would like to tell you the story of Two Twist. It was one of the first stories I was ever taught in my tribe. If you listen to the story, you will understand why I think the way I do. It pretty much sums it up:

Long before the United States had conquered the western half of the United States, when our tribe was roaming free, there was a man and his name was Red Robe. Red Robe lost two sons in a conflict with our enemy the Crow. Because of this, he gave all that he had away. He was in mourning. He had a lot of horses, a lot of wealth for the time. He had a prominent family. He was an elder who was revered in the tribe. He gave everything away. He didn't want anything. He pretty much lived homeless.

The warrior societies in our tribe—the Bow String, the Fox, the Dog Soldiers, the Elk—they all came together and asked him to come back to the camp. Because he was living on the outskirts, away from the people. He didn't want to be a part of people's life.

They came together and honored this elder and asked him to come back. He still refused. He said that his sons had died and he was in mourning for them. The societies told him, "Your sons died in the best way that a Cheyenne ever could. And that is to die in battle. He didn't live to be an old man. He didn't live to die of sickness. Your sons died defending their people, their way of life, which is the warrior culture of our tribe."

There was a soldier, a leader of one of the societies, the Bow String Society. His name was Two Twist. Two Twist made a vow, a pledge that he would lead the tribe against the Crow. He would die in battle. This would be the last battle on earth. All the tribe at that time vowed to go with him when he made this pledge.

The tribe moved against the Crow in mass formation. Two Twist led the Cheyenne against the Crow. And the Crow scouts saw they were coming and dug in. They knew they were surrounded in this valley where they were at. The Cheyenne let up. Two Twist led the tribe. He sang his war songs. His Bow String war songs. Made his pledge that he would never walk on this earth again. And all he had was a weapon that he had captured from the enemy. He had a saber. And he led the tribe into battle on his pony with this saber, and nothing else. He charged into the Crow. And he made all the rest of the people stay back until he went first into the fight.

He jumped into the breastworks of the Crow and fought by himself. The people saw him go down in the dust. He was dragged down as he was fighting his way through the enemy. At that time, the Cheyenne moved forward, surrounded the Crow and scattered the Crow to the wind. And beat back their enemy and destroyed them.

Two Twist lived through this battle. They found him, and he was still alive. From that day on, he was revered as a great warrior and a tribal leader. Which he became later on in life. The people never let him fight again because he had made this vow for another man.

Red Robe took him as his son. Red Robe honored him. Red Robe told the rest of the people that in this way you honor those who go to combat for you, that go to war for you.

By telling you this story, I want to show you that we as native people, as Cheyenne, still do that to this day. People such as myself and my family and my loved ones and people I know have come forth to represent our country in times of need like this. When we come back home, our families carry on that tradition that Red Robe did. He was honored that Two Twist went to fight for him, to die for him. In this way, you give them honor, the support, the recognition they need. Just as in the old days. Two Twist was one of the greatest warriors our tribe has ever known. Because of this, our people move forward in that same fashion to this day.

Specialist William Estevan (Acoma Pueblo) during drumming/singing practice at Camp Cropper, Iraq.

Right: Before a ceremony honoring Native Americans in the armed forces, General Douglas Stone speaks with Sergeant Dominick La Fontaine about the pronunciation of Navajo words to be incorporated into his speech.

This page and following spread: Native American Appreciation Month ceremony held at Saddam Hussein's main palace, Al Faw, at Camp Victory.

Lieutenant Bill Cody Ayon (left) and General Douglas Stone speak at Native American Appreciation Month ceremony.

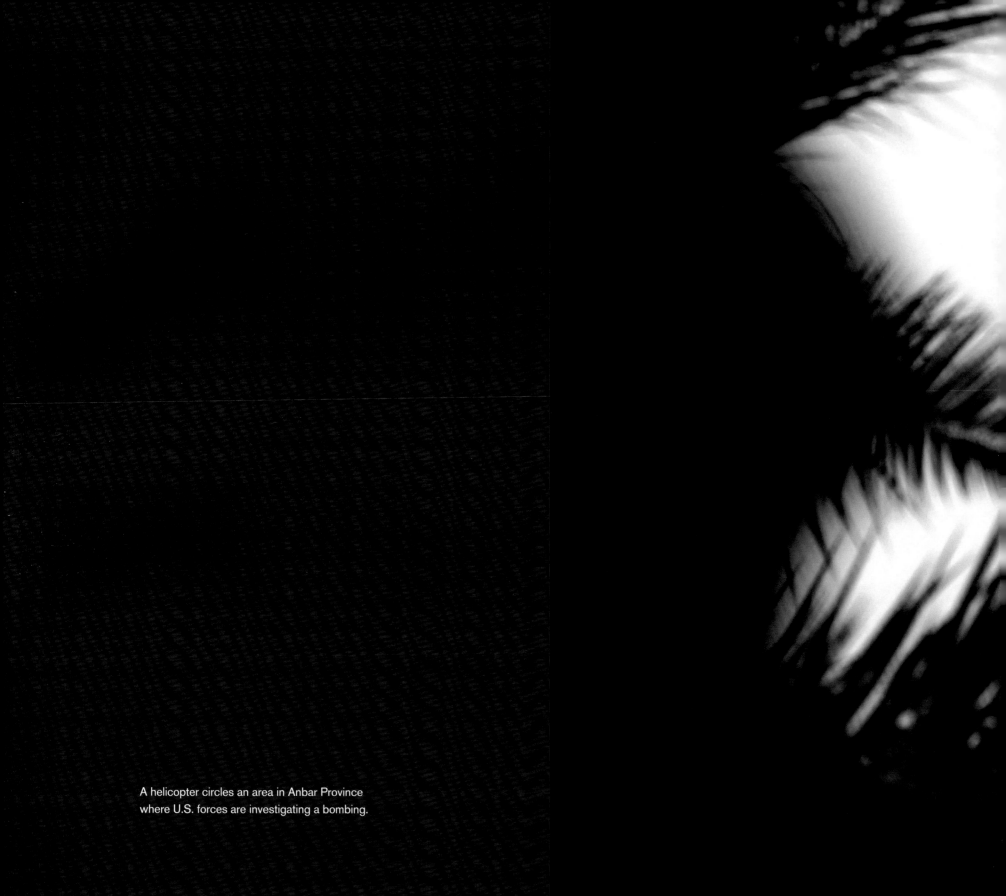

A helicopter circles an area in Anbar Province
where U.S. forces are investigating a bombing.

An Iraqi girl exits a bus that carried her and other visitors from meetings with relatives being held by U.S. forces.

Below: An Iraqi woman exits the bus used to transport her from the visitor center. From this location she will exit the base.

An Iraqi woman walks past a recently whitewashed wall surrounding a market in Baghdad.

An Iraqi woman fights back tears as she relates her story. While advancing toward the sound of an explosion, members of the First Squadron, Third Brigade Combat Team encountered terrified women and children running in their direction. The family claimed that an unknown individual had threatened them with violence if they didn't vacate their home. The blast was the third attempt to intimidate the family into leaving. Soldiers investigated the incident, but the outcome was inconclusive. The family returned to their home.

Army Sergeant Bradley Henio, New Mexico National Guard
Interviewed November 25, 2006, Ramah Navajo Reservation, New Mexico

Before you get back, before you start mingling with your family and everybody else, they do a singing and blessing and prayer for you. You try to cleanse yourself before you spread that among your family; kind of cleanse yourself until you have a bigger ceremony, a bigger prayer service. But this is just a small one that they do for you, a quick one when you come back. They do this for most veterans.

In the Native American Church they have what they call a prayer meeting. An all-night thing with prayers, and they have the Enemy Way ceremony, to get rid of all your bad experience. The next one is the Beauty Way ceremony, which is all the good things brought back to you or things left for you. So there are a lot of different versions.

It does help you. It's hard to explain. When I first got back I was filled with anger and stuff like that. I was kind of going the wrong way. My family and my brother, they all got a prayer and asked for forgiveness through the different fireplaces of the spirit world. And you try to confront your whole feelings just like a psychologist does. The medicine man talks with you all night, explaining the old folklore, the folk stories. My past history of my family, Navajo history. They use those stories to try to help you cope with your problem.

A native woman welcomes her veteran son, returning home after deployment to Iraq.

Native people welcome returning veterans, November 10, 2006, Gallup, New Mexico. All members of the 116th Transportation Company, New Mexico National Guard, returned from their yearlong deployment to Iraq.

A Navajo girl shouts that the honored Iraq War veterans have arrived. This welcoming-home celebration was held at the Ramah Chapter House on the Ramah Navajo Reservation in October 2006.

Family members at a homecoming for returning
Iraq War veterans in Gallup, New Mexico.

Family members anxiously wait for Iraq War veterans to arrive at a yellow-ribbon celebration at Rio Rancho High School. The returning vets are members of the 116th Transportation Company, New Mexico National Guard, based in Gallup, New Mexico.

A drumming group performs at a Gallup, New Mexico, homecoming celebration for returning veterans.

A Navajo elder enters the Ramah Chapter House to welcome Navajo veterans of the Iraq War.

World War II Navajo code talker Joe Vandever.

A Vietnam veteran sits and listens at a welcoming-home ceremony for Iraq War veterans at the Ramah Chapter House on the Ramah Navajo Reservation.

Dr. Mary Roessel
Interviewed January 27, 2009, Santa Fe Indian Hospital, Santa Fe, New Mexico

I would say that in the native culture there are roles that are pretty significant, and men need to assume certain roles. And I believe that if you've been in battle, if you've been in a war, when you come back you will be cleansed and you will be healed. There is a process for doing that. But then also there is a responsibility to assume more of a role within your community, because you've endured a lot, and you probably have a lot of wisdom from that as well.

I think that being a soldier is learned through so many different ways. In the Navajo culture, when the first twins had their Enemy Way ceremony they were examples of two different kinds of warriors. One went to war and fought and killed the monsters. He was called Monster Slayer. Then the other one, he was just as valued and necessary in these experiences in fighting. His name was Child Born for Water. He was the behind-the-scenes person. He was making the plans and strategizing. That example is very necessary when you talk to veterans or people who have been exposed to combat experience. There are two ways to be a warrior, and they were perfect examples of that. You have the Monster Slayer and the Child Born for Water. If you are not like one, you are like the other. So people can always associate with one of those types of warriors. They are very significant, and of course their mother, who was Changing Woman, is one of the most revered, holy people for the Navajo.

I think the warrior culture is a significant part of the Native American culture. In that warriors have been leaders. They have been peacemakers. They have been the ones who have guided our people in different ways. But I always think it is important when you are a warrior that you keep balance in your life. And that you are guided not so much by what you need to be doing but by your own holy people, the people you are representing who are guiding you.

Psychiatrist Dr. Mary Roessel works for the Indian Health Service in Santa Fe, New Mexico.

Jeanie Martine greets Iraq War veterans at a welcoming-home celebration at the Ramah Chapter House on the Ramah Navajo Reservation. Her nephew, Sergeant Bradley Henio, is pictured on page 88.

World War II Navajo code talker Joe Vandever
embraces an Iraq War veteran at a welcoming-home
and cleansing ceremony at the Ramah Chapter
House on the Ramah Navajo Reservation.

Iraq War veteran Bernard Henio embraces fellow veteran Joseph Martine at a homecoming
celebration for veterans at the Ramah Chapter
House on the Ramah Navajo Reservation. During the ceremony, the recently returned vets
lined up for greetings from tribal members and
area friends.

An Iraq War veteran embraces a fellow veteran at a homecoming celebration at the Ramah Chapter House on the Ramah Navajo Reservation.

Left and below: The Southern Tribe drumming group performs at a welcoming-home celebration at the Ramah Chapter House on the Ramah Navajo Reservation. The group played flag songs, victory songs, and honor songs.

Right: Veteran Joe Vandever speaks about the cleansing ceremony he is about to perform on returned Iraq War veterans. Vandever will use an eagle feather to spread smoke from burning incense over the returning veterans. Later, some members of the audience will participate in the same ceremony.

Sergeant Bradley Henio addresses the audience at a welcoming-home celebration held in his honor at the Ramah Navajo Reservation. Below: Sergeant Bailey Henio.

Opposite: Sergeant Bradley Henio is embraced at the celebration for his safe return from his second deployment to Iraq with the New Mexico National Guard. The man to his left collects contributions for the visiting drumming and singing group.

Beverly Charlie
Interviewed January 29, 2009, Farmington, New Mexico

My name is Beverly Charlie, and I am Navajo. I'm from a family of eight. Four brothers, four sisters. My mom raised us. Not necessarily the old traditions, but we still abide in and know some of the traditions. I'm the first out of my family who has joined the military. I'm pretty much the first and last so far.

I would see warriors—a bunch of guys would come out. Our native warriors. Where are the women? I think as time kept going, girls are as good as guys. Girls are trying to be equal to men. And I think I'm growing up with a newer generation, too. I thought, I want to be one of those people. I want to be able to hold the flag. I'm hearing in some powwows that women cannot hold the staff when they bring the flag in.

Why not? She was in the same war he was in. I went to Iraq just like the next person went to Iraq. How come I can't hold the staff? I think I would like to be that person, too. Especially if I can deploy just as much as him. I've seen people who have probably been in the military the same amount of time I have and have never been deployed. I see some males come in this office, and they look at me as if I've never been in the military. And I tell them I was in Iraq. Where have you been? And I start naming all these places and tell them, this is how many times I've deployed. They kind of back off, and they talk to me differently after that. And we are best friends again. And you can see the big difference.

Former army sergeant and Navajo tribal member Beverly Charlie.

Singers perform during a welcoming home celebration held for returning Iraqi veterans
at the Ramah Chapter House on the Ramah Navajo Reservation.

Father and son members of a drumming and singing group pray during a welcoming home
celebration held for returning Iraqi veterans at the Ramah Chapter House.

Two area residents listen as Navajo veterans are honored during a welcoming home celebration held at the Ramah Chapter House.

Right: A Ramah area resident prays during a welcome home celebration for Navajo veterans returning from deployment to Iraq.

Bailey Henio holds three photos. In his right hand is a photo of his warrior grandfather, Jose Pino. In the center is a photo of Henio as a young soldier during World War II. The third photo shows his father, Jake Henio.

Bailey Henio, veteran
Interviewed December 17, 2006, Ramah Navajo Reservation

They make a little pouch with the corn pollen, and I don't know what else they had in there. And the live eagle feather. Not the big long one but the little white feathers that were inside there too. They told us if you get captured or something like that this little feather is going to get you out of there. During the [Normandy] invasion, the landing craft stopped right there in the water, and the shore was way over there. I had to jump into the water and swim up, and I still had that rifle. I carried the rifle. And that little pouch got all soaked up with water. I carried it through and brought it back home.

When we got into the army, that's when we got to know each other. Navajos, Pueblos, Zunis. Three guys from Zuni. I asked about these men not long ago, and they told me they passed away. And there is one still living, and he is an old, old man. Another one from Jemez. He came around one time. He met me. He came over to where I was working. He told me where he lives, and he wants me to come and see him. I don't know if he is living or not.

All I know is that we were in a war. When the Japanese bombed Pearl Harbor, and Adolf Hitler declared war on the United States. We didn't have communication or radio or TV at that time around here. Nothing. We were way out here in the country. All I know, you are in the army. You are drafted now. You go.

They just told us to report to Gallup. You're old enough to be drafted. So we went to Gallup and had our physical.

They told us we should go home for two weeks and come back in two weeks. So we came home. We just hitchhiked, no vehicles at that time. In two weeks we went back again. And they sent us to Santa Fe. We got some people from Louisiana, all over Texas, everybody.

The physical was in a big gym. There were doctors all the way around, sitting along the walls. As we come in, they say take your clothes off. So we stood naked all around there. Some were looking at our eyes. The next one maybe your ears. All the way around. And they said put your clothes back on. We went into another gym there. Not everybody. They called names. Some go this way. There was a big bunch on both sides. They told this other group, you didn't qualify. I was with the other group, and they say, "Raise up your hands." So they swore us in, and they say, "You're in the army now. You want to go right now? We put you on the payroll right now. Or else you go home for two weeks. And come back in two weeks."

The guys right there training us, they say, "You do this, you do this." Early in the morning they would get us up. We would have breakfast and come back. The first morning I went over there, and they put us in

the line. The first morning we had an inspection. The officer came around and looked at us. He came to me and asked me what's my name. He wrote my name. He wrote it down. After that, they call our name. He called us aside. He said, "you didn't button up your shirt or things like that. You go to the mess hall. You're going to be over there all day. KP." Peeled potatoes, washed dishes, wiping all the tables. I had to do it all day. It was the first and the last time I worked KP. After that I really take care of myself. See that my shoes were all polished.

Later they gave us a rifle. And they just kept showing us how to use a rifle. And how to disassemble. Then they blindfolded us, and they mixed all the parts. Okay, you put it back together. And we put it back together. Then they sent us out to the firing range to shoot. There was one guy, he was from Las Cruces. Him and I made the same score. The top scores. So we fire again, and he beat me. So he got the sharpshooter badge, and I took the marksman.

I was just a sheep herder. I was just blank when I went into the army. I didn't know nothing about war.

Bailey Henio, age eighty-three, walks through the pasture at his home to check on his grazing sheep. Henio fought on D-day at Omaha Beach and at the Battle of the Bulge. He was raised and still lives on the Ramah Navajo Reservation.

A Navajo veterans' cemetery outside Fort Defiance, Arizona.

The Warrior Dance introduces young men to the warrior culture. Here, a boy in tribal costume dances in honor of Lieutenant Bill Cody Ayon.

Lieutenant Bill Cody Ayon adjusts his blanket during a Warrior Dance held in his honor.
The colors indicate that Ayon is a gourd dancer. The dance was held at a National Guard armory
in Albuquerque, New Mexico, in 2008. A Southern Cheyenne tribal member, Ayon is a member of
both the New Mexico National Guard and the Deming Police Department.

Right: An honor guard consisting of Santa Domingo Pueblo members waits to present colors at
Lieutenant Bill Cody Ayon's Warrior Dance in 2008.

Left: Lieutenant Bill Cody Ayon is wearing a Bronze Star earned for his participation in a psy ops (psychological operations) assignment.

Above: The Gourd Dance blanket worn by Lieutenant Ayon displays military ribbons and awards. It is a military and civilian service history of the wearer. The patches are from Ayon's service in the navy and army. The Bronze Star is for running a psy ops (psychological operations) program in Iraq.

Sergeant (ret.) John Henry Mashunkashey
Interviewed June 8, 2007, War Mothers' Dance, Gray Horse, Oklahoma

Patriotism for the Native American Indian—what I was told as a young man was—the Native American was one of and actually the only one fighting for his own country that belonged to him in the beginning. We fought all the wars. We were even in the Boxer Rebellion. We have stories of them climbing the China Wall.

The Osage themselves, we don't have a memorial regarding our own people. But we do have two organizations within our districts, our reservation: the Gray Horse American War Mothers and the Hominy American War Mothers. These individuals were full-blood Osage women who had sons or daughters that served in the military. Each year they have what they call War Mothers' Commemoration. There are individual songs that have been made and composed for their loved ones, whether they be KIA, WIA, or still living. Each year they sing these songs, and the tribe gathers, and we come in and we observe them.

We honor them, and we pass that legacy onto veterans that are getting ready to go to war. Whether it be in my era, the sixties, or now in the days of Iraq, Iran, and Kuwait. They are invited to come to the dance. At that particular time, they are recognized. Sometimes they have an honor song, a prayer song for that individual. And it's observed, and people come up to shake their hands and cry, mourn, or just tell them that they are in approval of their uniform. They are serving their country. They are serving their tribe.

When I came home from Vietnam they put me on a pedestal like they did the victory parades in World War II for my dad. When I came back, we couldn't even wear our uniforms in public. They told us to take them off. Native Americans are the only group of individuals, indigenous people that observe before and after, whether you lose, win, or die. It goes a long way to make you feel better.

Female Osage tribal members wear shawls and participate in the annual War Mothers' Dance held at Gray Horse, Oklahoma. The War Mothers Society was started by mothers of sons serving in the military during World War II. The mothers honor their relatives by displaying and wearing shawls during dances. Decorations on the shawls include chapter names, names of veterans, and service affiliations.

Amer
War M
Mi - Tho -
Chapt
Homin

AMERICAN WAR MOTHER
Mi-tho-ti-moi
Chapter 6
Hominy, OK

Angel

Osage tribal member Randoff Crawford leads a flag-carrying procession into the dance arena.

111

Osage tribal member and Vietnam veteran John Williams raises the American flag at the dance arena.

112

Osage tribal member and Vietnam veteran John Henry Mashunkashey. After two and a half years in Vietnam, Mashunkashey came home to a people who welcomed him and a nation that did not.

A man holds the flag during the War Mothers' Dance.

113

Corporal (ret.) Jessie Davis, Marine Corps
Interviewed November 24, 2008, Pawhuska, Oklahoma

A lot of people said bad things about Vietnam at the time. I did it because I thought it was the right thing to do.

I'm approaching sixty-two, and I've studied my own culture. And there are thirteen different rites that an Osage man had to go through before he became a respected warrior. Parts of them were killing a deer, a cougar, a bear. But also actions in combat—war, as you might say. And I have this inherent feeling that is part of what instilled me to do this. Why else would I want to go into combat for a country that basically tried to and wanted to annihilate my people? I think it maybe was Andrew Jackson, whose basic foreign policy with the Indians was, "The only good Indian is a dead Indian."

When I came back, it was not something I was ashamed of. However, because of the times and the political environment, only among my own people did I say I was a Vietnam veteran. And in the rest of the world, I did not say it. I did not deny it. But I did not come out and say that I was a Vietnam veteran. Not for a long, long time.

When I was fifty years old, I was designated to carry the flag on Veterans Day, at an age when I should have had plenty of confidence. But also I had a three-year-old daughter, the only child I've ever had. And carrying this flag was a great honor, a very prestigious honor. When you are outside an arena, you go clockwise. When you are inside the building, you go counterclockwise. I was very concerned whether I was going the right way, if I was holding the flag the right way, if I was going to drop it, or do this or do that. All of a sudden, my uncles Kenneth Jump, Franklin No Ear, they were right there with me. It was like a dream. They helped me stand straighter—at fifty years old I had a degenerating joint disease, so I hurt all over. As I just got started and was standing up straight and was worried about everything else, I felt at my right knee, my pants leg, I felt a tug and a pull. As I looked down, there was my three-year-old daughter dancing with me in step. All my uncles, my aunts, my grandparents, everyone before me, I could see them helping me and guiding me and my daughter. And afterward I knew this to be true because there were older Osage women who were very, very critical and critiqued all the other dancers. They asked me how long had I been working with my daughter to teach her to dance, because she did everything so perfectly and was perfection. They thought I was lying to them when I said, "I didn't even know she could dance." And I asked her mother, "Why did you send her out there?" She said, "I did not do that. She just took off and said, 'I'm supposed to be with my dad. I'm going.'" So call it whatever it was. I call it inherent feelings and think it's not so much in your blood but it's in your heart. I'm so proud of my daughter because she has that pride which I have, which my forefathers had. That is one of the reasons we stood up and decided, this is the way it is and we are warriors. We are going to stand up for what is right.

Vietnam veteran Jessie Davis assists his nephew Chakota Mays, age twelve, with his costume before an Osage tribal dance at Gray Horse, Oklahoma.

Corporal Hollis Stabler, Marine Corps
Interviewed June 10, 2007, Gray Horse, Oklahoma

My father served in World War II. He landed in North Africa as a tank commander with Patton. He got wounded and was transferred to Darby's Rangers in Sicily. He went to the French campaign in the French Riviera and then was sent to Anzio. He was wounded again at Anzio and was shipped back home. So my father had a warrior tradition. My father came back a decorated warrior with the Bronze Star, and my uncle Robert Stabler, who was killed at Anzio, was awarded the Bronze Star and the Silver Star. I was very conscious of the fact that my father was a decorated warrior. I watched him be esteemed by not only his people but also the Osage people down here in Pawhuska. I know very well from my history, the Omaha history, about the traditions of war. There is no doubt that it influenced me.

You have to know where you came from to know where you are going or where you are in the future. When a young boy was initiated as a man of the tribe, he was told his life was not his own. His life is in God's hands, and there is no need to be afraid of anything. He was there to protect the tribe and the people. For the Omahas, there are two kinds of war. One, when we are attacked and everyone stands and defends themselves. The other is when we go after somebody for revenge because of a previous attack or to steal horses or whatever. In this second case, the Council of War had to give its approval.

When I went into the Marine Corps, I knew my father had taught me a lot. We had hunted together. He had talked about his brother and his brother's death. I made the decision to enlist on my own. It is not our way to have a big to-do about it when you go. Before I joined, I went to tell my father. He was an industrial arts teacher and was sanding a board. When I told him I had enlisted in the marines, he said, "That's a good outfit." He never even missed a stroke. I went home and told my mom I joined the marines. She said, "You're crazy!"

Vietnam veteran Hollis Stabler stands outside his home on the Osage Reservation in northeastern Oklahoma. Hollis is wearing the scarlet colors of the U.S. Marine Corps.

Supporters await the return of New Mexico National Guard to their armory in Rio Rancho, New Mexico, March 2008.

118

In preparation for a welcoming-home feast for Sergeant Patrick Toya, relatives hang a sign of welcome outside Jemez Pueblo.

Lieutenant Isac Tenorio (center) exits a bus delivering soldiers to the ceremony for a New Mexico National Guard unit after its deployment to Iraq.

Sergeant Patrick Toya is greeted by his aunt at a welcoming-home feast in his honor at Jemez Pueblo. Toya had returned safely from a deployment to Iraq several months earlier.

At Jemez Pueblo, Sergeant Patrick Toya's family prepares a welcoming-home feast to celebrate his safe return from deployment to Iraq several months earlier. Left to right: Bertilla Gachupin Toya, Delia Gachupin, Angela Greer, and Bernice Gachupin.

Project director: Mary Wachs
Art and production: David Skolkin
Printed in Singapore
10 9 8 7 6 5 4 3 2 1

Library of Congress Cataloging-in-Publication Data
 Clevenger, Steven.
America's first warriors : Native Americans and Iraq / by Steven Clevenger.
p. cm.
ISBN 978-0-89013-564-8 (clothbound : alk. paper)
1. Iraq War, 2003—Participation, Indian. 2. Iraq War, 2003—Personal narratives, American. 3. Indian soldiers—New Mexico. 4. Indian veterans—New Mexico. 5. Indians of North America—Warfare. 6. Indians of North America—Rites and ceremonies. 7. New Mexico. National Guard. I. Title.
DS79.764.U6C58 2010
956.7044'340923970789—dc22

                                                              2009041537

Museum of New Mexico Press
Post Office Box 2087
Santa Fe, New Mexico 87504
www.mnmpress.org